Industry Changes America

Emily Laber

PICTURE CREDITS

Cover, pages 4, 5, 6-7, 12, 14-15, 25 (top left), 25 (bottom left and right), 26-27 (top), 28 (top), 31 (center right), 31 (bottom left), 34-c, 35-a, 35-b © The Granger Collection, New York; title page, pages 2-3, 13, 19, 20, 22-23, 31 (top right), 35-c courtesy Library of Congress; pages 8 (top), 14 (inset), 18, 21, 36 © Corbis; pages 8 (bottom), 16-17, 18-23 (borders), 28 (bottom), 30 (top), 31 (top left), 31 (center left), 32, 34-a © Bettmann/Corbis; pages 9, 25 (top right), 34-d © Collection of the Hudson Mohawk Industrial Gateway, Burden Iron Works Museum, Troy, New York; pages 10, 34-b © G.E. Kidder Smith/Corbis; pages 11, 30 (bottom), 35-d illustration by Hank Iken; page 16 (inset) © American Textile History Museum; 26 (bottom) © Eliot Cohen; 27 (bottom) © Lowell National Historical Park; page 29 © Granata Press/The Image Works; page 31 (bottom right) © Carl & Ann Purcell/Corbis; page 33 (left) *The Industrial Revolution* by Susan Washburn Buckley, © 2002 National Geographic Society, photos © New Bedford Whaling Museum, Old Dartmouth Historical Society, (inset) The Granger Collection; page 33 (center) *Building the Transcontinental Railroad* by Monica Halpern, © 2002 National Geographic Society, photos © Union Pacific Historical Collection, (inset) Abby Aldrich Rockefeller Folk Art Center, Williamsburg, VA; *The Age of Inventions* by Ann Rossi, © 2002 National Geographic Society, photos © U.S. Dept of the Interior, National Park Service, Edison National Historic Site, (inset) Museum of the City of New York/Corbis.

Produced through the worldwide resources of the National Geographic Society, John M. Fahey, Jr., President and Chief Executive Officer; Gilbert M. Grosvenor, Chairman of the Board; Nina D. Hoffman, Executive Vice President and President, Books and Education Publishing Group.

PREPARED BY NATIONAL GEOGRAPHIC SCHOOL PUBLISHING

Ericka Markman, Senior Vice President and President, Children's Books and Education Publishing Group; Steve Mico, Senior Vice President, Editorial Director, Publisher; Francis Downey, Executive Editor; Richard Easby, Editorial Manager; Anne Stone, Lori Dibble Collins, Editors; Bea Jackson, Director of Layout and Design; Jim Hiscott, Design Manager; Cynthia Olson, Art Director; Margaret Sidlosky, Illustrations Director; Matt Wascavage, Manager of Publishing Services; Sean Philpotts, Jane Ponton, Production Managers; Ted Tucker, Production Specialist.

MANUFACTURING AND QUALITY CONTROL

Christopher A. Liedel, Chief Financial Officer; Phillip L. Schlosser, Director; Clifton M. Brown III, Manager

CONSULTANT AND REVIEWER

Sam Goldberger, professor emeritus, Capital Community College, Hartford, Connecticut

BOOK DESIGN/PHOTO RESEARCH

Steve Curtis Design, Inc.

◀ A young girl learns how to run machinery in a cotton mill.

Contents

Copyright © 2006 National Geographic Society.
All Rights Reserved. Reproduction of the whole or any part of the
contents without written permission from the publisher is prohibited.
National Geographic, National Geographic School Publishing,
National Geographic Reading Expeditions, and the Yellow Border
are registered trademarks of the National Geographic Society.

Published by the National Geographic Society
1145 17th Street N.W.
Washington, D.C. 20036-4688

ISBN: 0-7922-5448-1

2014
5 6 7 8 9 10 11 12 13 14 15

Printed in Mexico

Life on the

In the mid-1700s, England had colonies in North America. Most people in these colonies lived on farms. Families worked together. They grew the food they ate. They made the clothes they wore. They made the things they needed. A hundred years had passed since the colonies were started. Yet daily life had barely changed.

▲ Many women in the 1700s made thread on a spinning wheel powered by a foot pedal.

Farm

▲ Farmers harvested their
crops by hand in the 1700s.

Big Idea
The Industrial Revolution changed the way people lived and worked.

Set Purpose
Learn about the Industrial Revolution.

A Cha

Questions You Will Explore

What was the Industrial Revolution?

How did the Industrial Revolution change people's lives?

ging World

M any changes were taking place in the United States at the end of the 1700s. One of the biggest changes had to do with how things were made. People had been making things with simple **machines** at home. Now people started making things with power machinery.

Using power machinery to do work changed the way people lived. For example, fewer people lived on farms. More people worked in **industry**, making things. These changes started in the late 1700s. They ended in the mid-1800s. This time is called the **Industrial Revolution.**

machine – a device made of moving parts that makes work easier

industry – a business related to making things

Industrial Revolution – the time between the late 1700s and the mid-1800s when the introduction of power machinery changed life in America

◄ These women are using machines to make cloth.

Made by Hand

Before the Industrial Revolution, people made things by hand. If your horse needed shoes, you took it to a **blacksmith.** A blacksmith made iron shoes for your horse's hoofs.

The blacksmith did every part of the job. He heated the iron. He hammered it into shape. He punched nail holes in the iron. Making a horseshoe by hand took a long time. A blacksmith could not make very many horseshoes in a day.

....
blacksmith – a person who works with iron

▼ **A horseshoe**

▲ **A blacksmith made horseshoes one at a time.**

Made by Machine

The Industrial Revolution changed the way horseshoes and other products were made. For example, in 1835, Henry Burden built power machinery for making horseshoes. One machine cut metal to the right size. Another machine punched holes where the nails would go. A third machine bent the metal into the right shape.

▼ **This machine could make 60 horseshoes every minute.**

New Factories

The new machines were too big to be used at home. They were put in large buildings called **factories.** One kind of factory made cotton into cloth. These factories were called **textile mills.**

factory – a building where products are made with power machinery

textile mill – a factory where cloth is made

▲ Factories were built next to rivers.

Powered by Water

Most mills were powered by water. They were built alongside fast-moving rivers and streams. The river water turned a large **waterwheel.** Big belts connected the waterwheel to the machines. When the waterwheel turned, so did the belts. The turning belts powered the machines.

....
waterwheel – a wheel turned by water and used to power machines

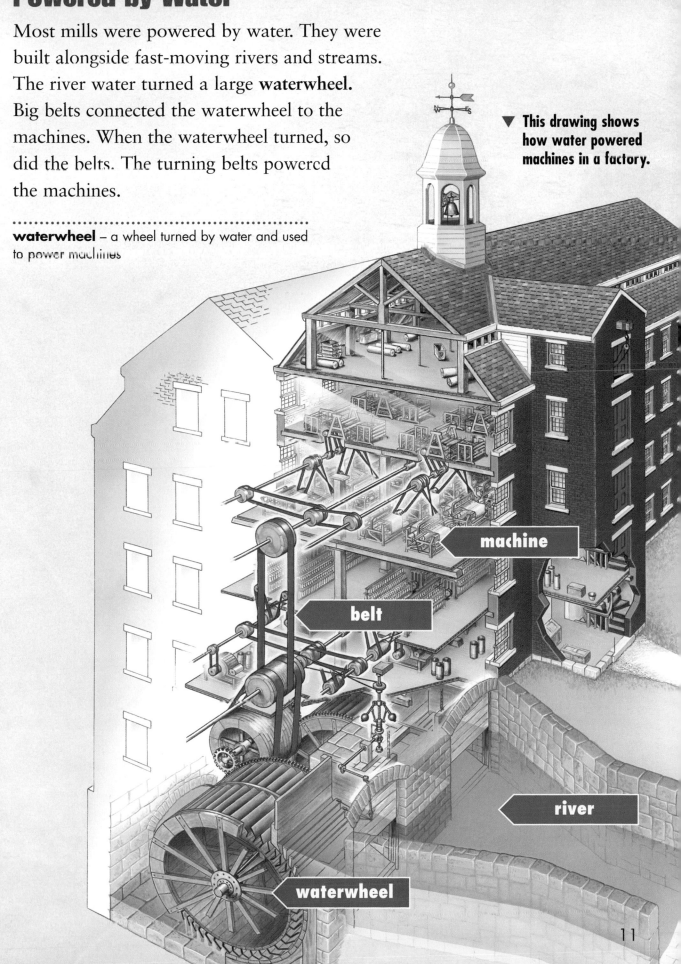

▼ **This drawing shows how water powered machines in a factory.**

machine

belt

river

waterwheel

Mill Workers

Many people worked in the textile mills. Some workers ran the machines that turned cotton into thread. Other workers ran machines that wove the thread into cloth. Still others fixed the machines.

▼ **Factory workers worked on different machines.**

Dangerous Work

Many mill workers were women and children. Some were as young as seven. These people worked long hours for little pay. The work was hard and dangerous. Factories were often unsafe and unhealthy. Many workers were hurt doing their jobs. Others got sick.

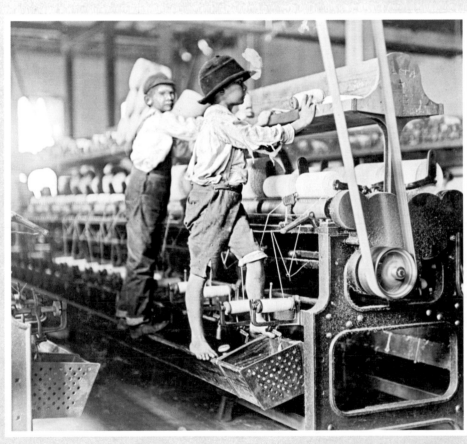

▲ Some boys were so small they had to climb on the machines to fix them.

Factory Towns

Before the Industrial Revolution, most people lived on farms. That changed when factories were built. Many factory owners built towns around their factories. They built houses and stores. Many people moved into these towns to be close to work.

▶ Workers lived close to the factories so they could walk to work.

Building America

The Industrial Revolution caused many changes in America. It changed the way people lived and worked. More people worked in factories and stores. More and more people lived in cities and towns.

These changes helped shape the world we live in today. People could now make goods quickly and cheaply. This helped the United States grow into a powerful country.

Stop and Think!

What changes did the Industrial Revolution cause?

▼ Towns grew up along rivers during the Industrial Revolution.

15

A Mill

Recap
Explain the importance
of the Industrial
Revolution.

Set Purpose
Meet a girl who worked
in a textile mill.

Girl

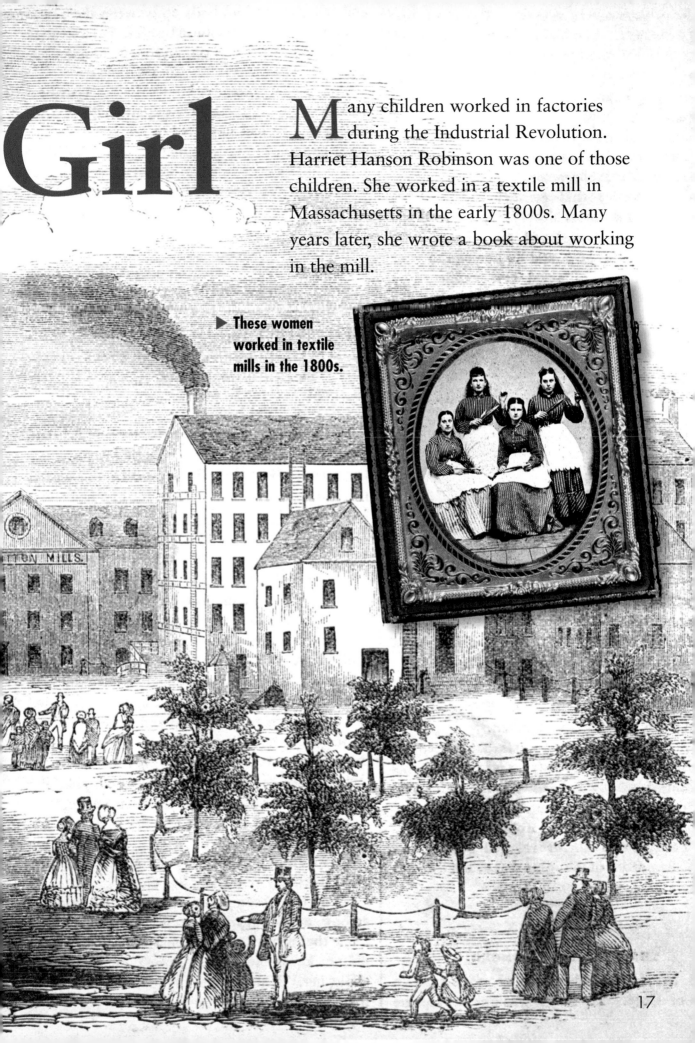

Many children worked in factories during the Industrial Revolution. Harriet Hanson Robinson was one of those children. She worked in a textile mill in Massachusetts in the early 1800s. Many years later, she wrote a book about working in the mill.

▶ **These women worked in textile mills in the 1800s.**

▲ This young girl ran a spinning machine in a mill.

Children's Work

Harriet wanted to help her family by getting a job in a textile mill. At first, her mother said, "No." She knew that working in a mill was dangerous. Finally, Harriet's mother agreed to let her daughter work in a mill. Harriet was 10 years old.

Harriet's first job was to remove thread from a machine. Young workers usually did this job. It was easy and safe. Harriet did harder and more dangerous jobs when she got older.

▲ **A girl needed a break from running loud and dirty machinery.**

Long Days

Harriet worked hard. She got to the mill at 5:00 in the morning. She stayed until 7:00 at night. She worked every day but Sunday. But she did not make much money. She made only $3.40 a week.

The machines made lots of noise. It was hard to hear over the noise of the machines. The air in the mills was full of dust. Some workers got sick from breathing the dusty air.

Mill Workers

Harriet met many other young women at the mill. Many of them needed money to help their parents run farms. Some came to America from other countries to look for work.

▲ Mill girls walked to work.

Proud to Be a Mill Girl

Not everyone thought girls and women should work in mills. They believed that girls and women should stay home. Harriet did not care. She thought it was important to make money to help her family.

Opportunities for Women

Harriet did not work in the mill her whole life. Like many other girls, she stopped working when she got married. She was 23 years old at the time. But she always remembered her years at the mill.

Working in the mills helped many women. It gave them **opportunities** they did not have before. For example, they earned money. This helped many women try other new things.

....

opportunity – a chance to do something

Stop and Think!

HOW did the Industrial Revolution change Harriet's life?

▲ This woman operated a
machine that made cloth.

Recap

Tell about the life of
a mill girl.

Set Purpose

Learn more about how
the Industrial Revolution
changed America.

CONNECT WHAT YOU HAVE LEARNED

The Industrial Revolution

The time between the late 1700s and the mid-1800s is often called the Industrial Revolution. During this time, machines were built that made making products easier and cheaper. Machines changed the way people lived and worked.

Here are some ideas that you learned about the Industrial Revolution.

- Many people lived on farms before the Industrial Revolution.
- Power machinery enabled people to make goods cheaper and faster.
- Many women and children worked in factories.
- Towns grew up around factories.

Check What You Have Learned

How did the Industrial Revolution shape the way we live today?

▲ Farmers harvested wheat by hand.

▲ This machine could make 60 horseshoes in a minute.

▲ Women and children worked long hours in the textile mills.

▲ People lived in towns built around the factories.

River Power

People built lots of mills in New England during the Industrial Revolution. That is because New England has many fast-moving rivers. The mills needed rivers for power. New England's rivers made it a perfect place for the Industrial Revolution to begin in America.

▲ Most factories were built alongside rivers.

▲ The Boott Mill is now a museum.

Visit a Mill Town

The mills in Lowell, Massachusetts, were successful for many years. But most closed by 1930. Many of these mills are still standing. They have been turned into a museum.

The Boott Mill is one of the mills at the museum. Many of its machines still work. Water from a river turns the mill's waterwheel and powers the machines.

▲ **Weaving at Boott Mill**

Improving Factories

▲ **Model T Ford**

During the Industrial Revolution, machines made work faster and easier. In 1913, Henry Ford made factories better. He did this by giving each worker a different job.

Ford owned a car factory. He had his workers stand along a line. A car moved from worker to worker until it was finished. This setup is called a moving assembly line.

▲ **Workers build cars on the assembly line in a Ford factory.**

▲ **Robots build cars on this assembly line.**

More Machines Than Ever

Many factories still use the assembly line system. Often robots, not people, work on the assembly lines. A robot is a machine controlled by a computer.

Some robots do boring jobs. Other robots do dangerous jobs to help keep workers safe. Factories that use robots do not need to hire as many workers.

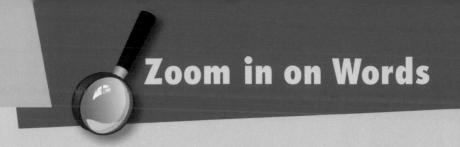
Many kinds of words are used in this book. Here you will learn about compound words. You will also learn about nouns.

Compound Words

Compound words are made by joining two shorter words. You can often figure out what a compound word means by knowing what the two shorter words mean.

horse + shoe = horseshoe

Blacksmiths made **horseshoes** one at a time.

water + wheel = waterwheel

A **waterwheel** powered the factory.

Nouns

A noun is a word that names a person, place, or thing.
Use the nouns below in your own sentences.

A **horseshoe** is made out of iron.

Harriet thought it was important to help her **family.**

These **buildings** belonged to the factory owner.

The mills needed fast-moving **rivers** for power.

The mills made cotton into **cloth.**

River water turned a large **waterwheel.**

Write About the Industrial Revolution

The first textile mill in North America opened in 1791. A man named Samuel Slater built it. Read more about Samuel Slater and his mill. Then write an essay about him.

Research

Collect books and reference materials, or go online.

Read and Take Notes

As you read, take notes and draw pictures.

Write

Then write an essay about Samuel Slater and textile mills.

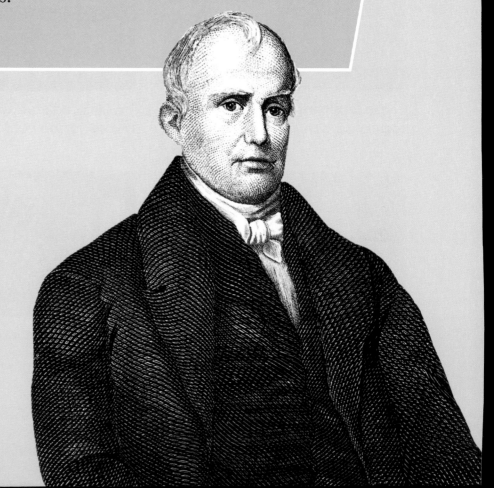

▶ Samuel Slater

Read and Compare

Read More About the Industrial Revolution

Find and read other books about the Industrial Revolution. As you read, think about these questions.

- What was life like before the Industrial Revolution?
- How did the Industrial Revolution change life in America?
- Which changes do you think were the most important?

Books to Read

▲ Discover how machines changed the way products were made.

▲ Learn how building the transcontinental railroad changed the country.

▲ Read about inventions that changed how we live and work.

Glossary

blacksmith (page 8)
A person who works with iron
A blacksmith made horseshoes.

factory (page 10)
A building where products are made with power machinery
The machines were kept in large buildings called factories.

Industrial Revolution (page 7)
The time between the late 1700s and the mid-1800s when the introduction of power machinery changed life in America
This period of change is called the Industrial Revolution.

industry (page 7)
A business related to making things
More people worked in industry.

machine (page 7)

A device made of moving parts that makes work easier

People started using machines to make products.

opportunity (page 22)

A chance to do something

Working in the mills gave women new opportunities.

textile mill (page 10)

A factory where cloth is made

Textile mills were one kind of factory.

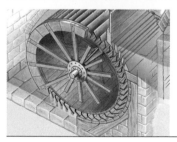

waterwheel (page 11)

A wheel turned by water and used to power machines

The river water turned a large waterwheel.

Index